Friendship with the Elements
OPENING THE CHANNELS OF COMMUNICATION

By Don Alverto Taxo

Compiled & Edited by Helen Slomovits

LITTLE LIGHT PUBLICATIONS
2000 Penncraft Ct.
Ann Arbor, MI 48103

LITTLE LIGHT PUBLICATIONS
2000 Penncraft Ct.
Ann Arbor, MI 48103
(734) 665-0409
helens22@comcast.net

Editorial: *Helen Slomovits*
Cover Design: *Leisha Bell with Helen Slomovits*
Illustration: *Helen Slomovits*
Typography: *Leisha Bell*
Photo Credits: Front Cover - *Elizabeth Alberda*, Back Cover - *Susan Cooper*
Note from Don Alverto Photo - *©2002 Monte Fowler www.montefowler.com*
Other Photos - *Elizabeth Alberda, Carole Brill, Susan Cooper, ©Monte Fowler pp. 1 & 59, Nancy Harknett, Aileen Kernohan, Daniel, Laz & Helen Slomovits*

First printing, September 2005
Printed in USA
ISBN 978-0-9675933-3-3   (0-9675933-3-6)

Don Alverto Taxo
albertotaxo@hotmail.com

Acknowledgements

This book has been created with the love, time and contribution
of many people. I want to especially thank Martha Travers, Michael Smith, and
Carole Brill, all students of Don Alverto, for their many hours of
note taking and transcription of workshops with Don Alverto since 2000.
These form the pool from which this book is drawn.

I want to thank Marilynn Lutjens, my husband Laz Slomovits,
Carole Brill, Susan Cooper and Priscilla Dawes for their
editorial contributions, encouragement and belief in this book.

Many thanks to Susan Cooper, Monte Fowler, Aileen Kernohan,
Elizabeth Alberda, Nancy Harknett, Laz Slomovits and Daniel Slomovits who
shared their beautiful photos from trips to Ecuador, and from moments of daily
life seen with the eye of connection and
appreciation.

None of this would have been possible without the generosity
of heart and spirit, and the eloquence and simplicity of wisdom that
Don Alverto brings to each moment and to every encounter,
a small part of which is reflected here.

Helen Slomovits

Note from Don Alverto

I recommend that you read through the chapter
summaries in the Table of Contents first and choose the chapter
that attracts your attention and applies most to your current needs.
Then read the chapter you chose slowly and as many times
as you need to fully enjoy and appreciate it. Apply what you've read
in your daily life experiences as much as possible so you can
use it to really improve your life.
Say a prayer according to your beliefs or religion
asking that this practice benefit
every aspect of your life.

Table of Contents:

The Power of the Condor: the Power to Feel

*The time will come when the Eagle and
the Condor will fly together in the same sky.*
— PROPHECY OF THE KICHWA ELDERS

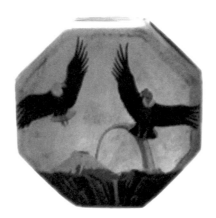

Eagle & Condor

WE ARE TOGETHER, the Eagle and the Condor. We have been together before, and it is no accident that we are together now. Our being together confirms the prophecies of our ancestors – that a time would come when the Condor, from the South, and the Eagle, from the North, would fly together in the same sky.

In this life, it is important to combine the gifts of the Eagle with the gifts of the Condor. We need both powers: the power of the Eagle – which is the power of the mind, including the gifts of science and technology, and the power of the Condor – which is the power of the heart, including the gifts of feeling and connection with the elements of the Earth.

These two powers – mind and heart, Eagle and Condor – are also inside us. They need to fly together inside each one of us. The power of the Eagle is to think and to plan. The power of the Condor is to feel and to connect. The sky is our daily lives. To fly is to enjoy each moment of our life, and from this experience of life, to continually and spontaneously express gratitude.

In the prophecies, it was said that when the Condor and the Eagle fly together in the same sky, there will be harmony.

What I'm bringing is the power of the Condor: the power to be able to feel – in every place, and in every moment. That is the power of the Condor of the Andes.

FEELING IS THE RESPONSE OF OUR WHOLE BEING, without interference from the mind or thought. By 'feeling' I mean that you perceive with attention, from the heart. The simplest way to develop our capacity to feel is through giving awareness and attention to the four elements — Earth, Air, Fire, Water.

To feel is a different function of the body than thinking. We feel more when we're more relaxed, not only in the body, but relaxed in our feelings and emotions and relaxed in our thinking.

The capacity to feel (sentir) differs from sensation and the five senses. We may touch with our fingers, but what we touch with them may be felt by the heart, from the heart. That is feeling.

When spring arrives, what do you feel? You don't have to think, in order to feel all that spring brings. You enjoy, you feel, you experience what spring brings. It's the same way when you have an intimate contact with the elements and with God. Then you are fulfilled and remain fulfilled.

Develop your power of feeling — all the time, more and more. It's simple. For example, taking a bath, we can feel the water caressing and cleansing our skin. "The power of water enters all my organs and makes me healthy. I am part of water and water is part of me. Water is Life and I am Life."

In this way we receive the power of water. It is the same with wind, air, fire, Mother Earth. The mind says, "When? Where?"

All the time. Everywhere.

The Great Mother Nature and the Great Spirit of Life, act for us through the elements of nature. That's why it's very necessary to have an intimate contact with Nature. It's not difficult. To think is difficult. To feel is natural. To think about wind is complicated. To feel wind is natural, easy. It is the same with the other elements – earth, fire, water.

We ourselves, we're part of Nature. Our mind understands this. Now we have to feel this truth. It's important to think and know this truth. But it's much more important to feel this truth.

There are many things we can know. But in this time – it's urgent to *feel* what we know. In order to *feel* what we know, we should practice and *feel* whatever it is that we're drawn to. For example, we know how important the air is. We may know its chemical and physical properties. A form of feeling air is to breathe, to be aware of breathing. Also when air is moving, to allow our body to be there and experience the air touching us. There are not many words to express the feeling of the experience of air. We each feel and experience air in our own way. Each of us should practice making good use of each element.

Up until 1989, the emphasis was on thinking. From 1989 and on, other things are rising — feeling is one. This is the responsibility of the Andes — to invite people to this path of feeling. It is not about a new religion or new techniques. It is an invitation to take advantage of what we already know — to feel more, to complete our life and to feel our life with more sense of purpose.

When we start feeling, this helps us realize — everything is sacred. In Kichwa there is no word for sacred or not sacred. We feel from the smallest to the greatest — everything is sacred. The whole is part of each one, and each one is part of the whole. My invitation to you is to begin anew and to increase your power to feel.

Friendship with the elements is a door you can enter to help you find the power of feeling.

2

My Culture, My Education

I thought the type of education that I received was natural to everyone. But when I met people from the city, I realized this wasn't so for everyone. They did not feel the water. They did not feel the Earth. They thought the water and the Earth had no life. So they could not imagine that they could communicate with them. That's when I realized it had been a great gift to receive this education.

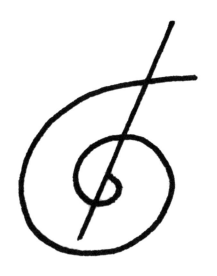

I'M FROM ECUADOR, from the Andes in Ecuador, in the middle of the earth, in South America. My culture is a root culture. It is pre-Inga (Inca). I belong to an indigenous nation, the Atis, the Kichwa (Quechua). Our traditions come from many, many years ago. Fifty years before the Spaniards came, the Ingas arrived. And we shared a lot of things with the Ingas who came from Cusco.

We have a concept of life that is different from modern life. This difference is valuable because it allows us to share with other cultures. As part of our cosmovision, we see life as a great circle. We don't see life as linear, beginning at one point and then going forward. *This circular concept of time and space allows us to integrate everything we do in life.*

Something simple that we may do in our daily lives may have an

important affect. For example, to visit a waterfall is very important to us. The waterfall is not only a physical phenomenon — a liquid. When we are with a waterfall we are being with life — with a distinct type of life. The waterfall is a being that communicates with us, and we can communicate back with it. Of course, it is natural that a waterfall does not communicate the way we do.

For example, we communicate with the water element by singing. This song we sing from the heart to communicate what we are feeling. We have observed that people who come from the city and who try to communicate with water, are *thinking* about communicating, whereas we are *feeling*.

For us it is very important to feel the communication, not only to think about it. We can use a song, we can use a chant, or we can use a different way of expressing what we feel, for example, by leaving gifts or "offerings".

The action of thinking is a characteristic of the Eagle. It is a power of the Eagle. The action of feeling is a characteristic of the Condor. It is a power of the Condor. It is good to think. It is good to feel. It is much better to feel and to think.

When we express how we feel to the water, this produces a special reaction in the water and it also produces a special reaction in us. For example, people who commu-

nicate this way feel peace and tranquility inside. And as the water is flowing, it begins to express more sounds. This is the way we and the water are communicating. We benefit mutually. The water benefits and we benefit. The same is true of earth, of air, and of fire.

When we have a problem that is very great, for example, we may go to the mountain to help us with this concern. We go to communicate with the Earth, with the rocks, so that we can discover what it is that is creating our disquietude.

I do not have words that are adequate for describing the type of communication that happens. It is a state that is related to feeling. But we believe it is something very important in our lives because it helps us in many ways.

Like everyone, we have things we want to learn about, things we want to know. To learn, we go to the elements, as I just explained with water. We can do the same with the wind, the earth, and fire — with whatever exists in nature.

Q: How do you know when you've made contact with nature and the elements?

A: You don't know with your head. You feel it. You feel fulfilled. You have met the water. It is natural for the mind to say, "What? You didn't hear anything!" It is possible that the mind will say, "You have not yet established communication because you haven't heard anything." But this type of communication gives one a special feeling of tranquility, and later, possibly, when you return to the house or the next day, a solution to the problem comes.

———

Q: How long have you been like this? Did you come to this at a certain age?

A: I don't know at what age, but my first memory of this is being with my grandfather and feeling this way. I remember that he took me to the mountain. He took me in his arms singing and carried me to a natural spring. He would sing to the water, saying, "Let us play with the children in the water." After a while, in reality, I was there in the water with many children. And then I was in a state of not really sleeping but somewhat like sleeping, and I was still in the arms of my grandfather. I had a very beautiful sensation of having played with the children that were in the water. As I grew up, it wasn't as much playing with the water as it was learning what the water had to say about life.

Q: How does this connection affect your life, how you see your life, and your work?

A: I hadn't noticed that it had a special impact on my life. I thought this type of education that I received was natural to everyone. But when I met people from the city, I realized this wasn't so for everyone. For example, they did not feel the water. They did not feel the Earth. They thought the water and the Earth had no life. So they could not imagine that they could communicate. That's when I realized it had been a great gift to receive this education.

———

Q: Given all the injustices done to your people, how is it that you can come from a place of the heart to offer the wisdom and gifts of your tradition to the people of the Eagle?

A: This is the value of the spiritual. The normal thing would not be to give more, because there has been and there still is a lot of unfairness towards my people. But injustice does not end injustice. Hate does not end hate. Darkness is ended with light and hate with love.

It is easy to give love to people that love us. However, it is possible and necessary to transmit love to people who have hurt us, because that is where the spiritual opportunity lies — to give love even though one might have received hate. There is where the merit lies. There is where our spiritual advancement lies.

Q. In your path how did you learn this?

A: The history of the native people after the arrival of the Spaniards is very, very hard and very ugly. When I was very young, I felt a lot of pain due to this reality. I couldn't understand very well my grandmothers and grandfathers, that they held so much love even for people who caused them so much pain. Sometimes I confused that with them being cowards, because they didn't respond in kind to injustices. I sometimes would stay up in the top of a tree looking at how few they were and how many we were and thinking how easy it would be for us to get together and destroy all of them — very easy.

One day I understood with a grandmother that life is not only this body and that there exists a great opportunity to move forward when we do not respond to hate with hate. When we give something beneficial we ourselves receive more benefits. I have proof of that every day in my life. Materially, I have lived on the street and when I have done something of benefit to another I have always received food or whatever I needed. And this understanding has continued to progress; the more I give, the more things I do to benefit others, the more benefits I receive. It is a permanent ascent.

IN MY TRADITION, the elder people are the light on our path. Our grandmothers and our grandfathers hold our way of life, the way of life that we journey.

The typical Andean family has the grandmother down to the grandchildren, all living in the same household. If a daughter gets married, her husband becomes part of the family. If a son gets married, his wife also becomes part of the family. In one house, lives a very large family. For us, that's very important. A big family is very important. Grandmothers have much to teach us. The grandchildren and the great grandchildren also have things to teach us. That's the school, the first great school of the family. Thanks to that tradition, our knowledge and our traditions have been able to be sustained.

We don't learn so much by listening, or because someone is teaching us by talking. We learn by observing, on a daily basis, what the elders do. We observe how nature transforms, day after day,

observing and feeling the different elements of nature. I don't remember that my grandfather taught me things, "Sit down, I'm going to tell you something." But my grandfather would invite me to come and do the things he was doing. I was very happy being permanently behind my grandfather. I wasn't thinking about how I would one day have the responsibility that I now have.

I wasn't thinking that I would be a Iachak*.

I wasn't prepared for that. I only remember that I really liked being behind my grandfather. And my grandfather was most assuredly very patient with me, supporting me all that time.

And that's how I started helping him, maybe when I was about seven, picking herbs with him. When somebody came to ask questions, or somebody was coming for a healing, I would stop playing or eating and run to be next to my grandfather. And that's how I learned, without consciously preparing myself to be a Iachak, and without being forced to learn. Then I became my father's helper. And later, my father sent me to live with other elders who were very wise, in Bolivia, Peru, Colombia and Mexico. So, I consider a natural education that's flowing to be very important.

Our traditions are directed towards harmony with all of existence. Everything that exists, everything that we see, is a manifestation of love — love towards the Great Spirit of Life. We ourselves are part of that Spirit of Love, of the Great Spirit of Life. So we should proceed daily according to this idea, this principle, through the principle of love.

* A Iachak is a leader of the community, someone whose responsibility is to help in all ways — spiritually and materially — to guide, to support, to advise, to heal, to uplift.

So then, how to live.

To love, first you have to feel. Love is not a word. Love is something spontaneous that comes from one's heart, without classifying it. In love it's not possible to say, "I love this, and I don't love that." You can't say, " I love this animal, but this other one, I don't love." Or, "I love my neighbor on the right, but I don't love my neighbor on the left."

It's very important in my tradition to have this harmony with everything in existence. Our grandfathers and grandmothers have shown us that in the same way that we give, we receive. And we're interested in receiving beautiful gifts. We want life to be very good to us. So we feel love and respect for everything in existence.

Personally, I don't share the opinion that minerals have no life, for example. For me, everything has life — different forms of life, different ways of expressing. The tree expresses itself. Rocks express themselves. The river expresses itself. The air expresses itself. The sun expresses itself. Everything that exists expresses itself, just like us. Just like us, because we're a part of this existence. An apple expresses

itself. It's the crystallization of Mother Nature's love.

So, one way of expressing love and giving that love to Mother Nature, is to feel love for what we eat — to eat with gratitude, to eat with feeling — not just to fill our bellies, mechanically. To feel love is to not throw away food, for example. If there's something you love, you can't waste and throw it away.

When you have love and gratitude for the gift of life in some-thing, you just can't throw a part of it away. In each grain of rice or a piece of lettuce, the power of creation exists. There's the love and wisdom of the Great Creator. In each person is the force of the Great Creator. This is one of the beliefs that has a lot of value in our tradition. This has allowed us to maintain our culture.

Gratitude

You know that in history indigenous people were not treated well. Up until now we have not had a just treatment. With all those problems, despite all those problems, we continue to practice feeling gratitude towards life. To cultivate corn, we express our gratitude to the Earth. To help it grow and take care of it, we also express gratitude. When we harvest it, we also show gratitude and we have celebrations, celebrations for which we prepare all the different types of corn in different dishes. We express gratitude with words or mentally, in silence through our intention.

Every activity in life is an opportunity to show gratitude, in a natural way. We shouldn't think that I *should* have gratitude. If I understand the love of nature, I don't need to think. It's spontaneous. It's necessary to have a spontaneous attitude of reciprocity with the gifts of nature.

And we shouldn't only give thanks for things we want in this moment, and only expect from life the things about which we say,

"I want this," and when we receive that, then we're a little bit grateful. We should also give gratitude for things that we don't understand, and that we don't like. For me, there's no punishment in creation. How many things that I don't like and that I reject, later, with time, I understand that they were necessary for me. Isn't that true? But even with that, sometimes we don't learn. We only want and ask for things that we like. And if the things that we want don't happen, then we think that the Creator is not listening to us. Maybe what we're asking for and what we want are not appropriate at this time. Maybe a child asks his mother or his father for a knife. Will the mother and father give him a knife? I don't think so. Maybe there are certain things that instead of elevating us spiritually and materially, will actually stop us. Is that possible?

In my tradition, there's no formal way for asking things of life. I've learned from my grandfathers and grandmothers simply to give gratitude for what I receive and what I don't receive. There are so many things that we receive, that there's no room to want anything else. Maybe some people are not aware of all the gifts they receive from the moment they wake up. And because they're not aware of it, and they're not conscious of it, they think they need more things and they ask for more. From my point of view, it's important to start to giving gratitude for the gifts that life has given us, with all our hearts, in a very sincere and spontaneous way.

For example, Life has given us sight. We can see. Let's give thanks because we can walk. Let's give thanks because we can breathe. Let's give thanks because we can feel different textures. Let's give immense gratitude because we can smell. I have met a lot of people who can't smell. What a lack those people have, for example, not being able to smell the essential oils. We can smell the fragrance of a rose. Let's give gratitude for all these great gifts that we have. We could spend all afternoon and all night, enumerating all the things that we can be grateful for. Isn't that true? So how could there be time to ask for more?

We also express gratitude through our songs. Happiness and joy is another way of giving gratitude towards life. Why should we be so serious? The body grows and time passes, but that doesn't mean we have to become so serious.

And let's not make our children serious. Happiness is a way of giving gratitude to life. Maybe children don't say "Thank you, thank you," but in their happiness and in their play, they're expressing gratitude towards life. Why force them to be too formal? In the Kichwa people, there isn't a lot of formality. In one household grandchildren, parents, grandparents, and great grandparents live together. So, everyone participates when there's talking. And when we go to harvest, the little ones, they come, they play, but they do something as well. And, then they are very happy when they say, "I helped plant this corn," when they're eating it. And through their happiness and joy while they're eating, they're giving gratitude to Mother Nature.

Some people at the table do a lot of praying. They finish praying and then they eat mechanically. They're thinking about other things, they're talking about other things, and they're eating mechanically. Their prayer was also mechanical. Let's not trick ourselves. Let's be natural. Let's be happy.

In my tradition, there's a custom to always have parties where the whole community participates.

The house is open, and everybody comes and eats and dances and participates. They're not invited. They just come. Everybody comes. That's the way we think of giving gratitude for what we receive from nature.

Let's reflect a little bit on what things we can give gratitude for, and let's practice giving gratitude. And little by little, we'll start to discover the wonderful existence around us. There will be obstacles and things that aren't agreeable to us, but they're part of life. And, if we give gratitude for those things that we don't like very much, that means we've made improvement. And I'm sure, that by feeling gratitude for a difficult moment, the difficulty disappears. It's possible that it's a lesson — not a punishment. In our tradition, there isn't a punishing God.

So, the way of life that we have

is a system of gratitude, multiple experiences and expressions of gratitude. And we receive more gifts because we understand life better. The greatest prayer of Life is permanent gratitude towards Life.

Joy and happiness are other great prayers of Life. Feeling gratitude when we're eating is another prayer. Taking a bath, feeling a sensation of gratitude towards the water, is another prayer. Walking, being aware of the fact that it is a great gift, is another prayer. It's very simple to have contact with the wisdom of the Creator.

To live feeling gratitude with all our hearts, every moment that we breathe, is it possible?

I feel gratitude for the opportunity that I have to speak with you. I have gratitude because of my grandfathers and grandmothers, who kept these traditions alive — very difficult in the time of the

invasion of the Spaniards — and transmitted them to future generations. This meeting shows me that the Eagle and the Condor are flying together.

The people of the north – you – represent for us, the Eagle. We believe ourselves to be people of the Condor. The prophesy of the elders says that one day, the condor and the eagle will fly together in the same sky. And now we're together flying in this dream of gratitude towards life. And for that I feel an immense gratitude, for this moment, and for this place. For you.

3

Intimate Contact with the Elements

*To connect with Mother Nature, it's necessary to greet her.
When we greet someone and they greet us, a connection
is made. The mind might say, "How should I greet?" The
heart knows how to greet. The heart greets according to
how it feels — spontaneously.*

IN MY TRADITION, it is very important to have very personal, very intimate contact with all the elements of nature that sustain our lives. This intimate relationship with the elements of life guarantees that our body has more life. This intimate relationship helps so that we have a life that is happier, more harmonious, and healthier. When we distance ourselves from the relationship with nature, we're in danger of having health and harmony problems.

It's a part of the Ecuadorian and Andean tradition, and it's part of the path to have a close relationship with nature so that this force of life and the Cosmos can come into us and fill us with more life. So that the harmony of the Great Creation of the Spirit will come into us, and will give us more happiness. So that the great Spirit of Life will be with us. So that we have a meaning in life. So that we don't lose our path.

When we have the path in front of us, with the intimate relationship with nature, each day of our life has meaning. Each moment of our life is an opportunity for discovery. Each moment of our life is an opportunity to live more fully. That's why, in our tradition, we put a lot of emphasis on the intimate contact with nature — with water, with earth, with air, with fire, and with the fifth element which we call Ushai.

Ushai is the result of the union of the four elements in harmony. When we have this fifth element in our life, we have a sense of harmony in life. If we eat something, we are conscious that it is earth that we are eating, and that earth nurtures this earth that we call the body. We are conscious that our body is earth walking. And this walking earth, we need it to be in harmony. We should not pollute the rivers that are in this walking earth. It is necessary that with this understanding of our contact with Nature, we use each moment in life to receive the powers of nature's elements, to heal our bodies, to heal our minds, to heal our emotions, and to fill our lives with happiness and meaning.

For example, when we take a shower we can have contact with water, not only to bathe our skin, but to feel the power of water, to let the power of water go into our pores. To allow the power of water to enter every place in our body. To allow all the negativity in us to go out of our body with the shower. To allow whatever we don't have to carry anymore, to go away with the water. Even with just the daily shower we can do a lot of things, if we do it with feeling, if we really feel it. If we take a shower in a mechanical way, then we're just going to feel our skin. It's also necessary to feel our interior.

We can also do something similar with the earth, to receive the power of the earth, the harmony of

the earth, the wisdom of the earth. How shall we do it? For example, when we eat. Because what we eat, it's earth. An apple is transformed earth. Lettuce is transformed earth. It's a transformation of the love from Mother Earth. It's not only an apple, it's not only lettuce. It's the love of Mother Earth. If we eat feeling this love, then we receive the benefits of our Mother. If we eat mechanically, then we only fill the stomach. If we eat with feeling, then we fill the heart; we nurture the spirit and also the body. These are simple things. We can all do them.

If we transform ourselves, as daughters, as sons, who receive the love of Mother Nature, and we also give that love to Mother Nature, then we'll have great benefits, because every mother wants the best for her children. Such is Mother Nature's love. We only need to be in her arms, to feel the intimate contact with our Mother Nature.

We can start connecting with any element — some people with water, others with fire, others with air, others with whichever element is closest to them. It's not a difficult thing. It's very simple. It's a natural thing. You don't need to read many books. You just need to feel, to feel more every day. You need to breathe the air, and to be grateful in your heart because each breath assures the life of this body. When we breathe, we breathe in

the power of Life. And if we are conscious of this gift of air, then we are filled with the wisdom of air.

There are many stories that we read, or are read to us when we are children. And we think they're fantasies. But they're true. It's a truth that we can live right now, too. We only need to feel. Each day, to feel more, that intimate contact with the elements of nature – when we eat, when we drink, when we shower, when we breathe, when we take in the sun, when we look at a flower, when we smell the smells of nature. There are many gifts that we can receive. They are for us, if we have our heart open.

Wisdom is not far away. Wisdom is not outside of us. Wisdom has always been with us. We only need to feel. To feel is a powerful key.

We feel that the contact with the elements of nature helps us a lot in our lives. And one way to make contact among people is the salutation. What do we do when we meet each other? We greet each other. That's exactly what we have to do with the elements of nature. We greet them with the heart, with the mind, with the body, with the eyes, with the ears. To listen to the symphony of nature is a way of greeting, too. To touch the earth, to smell the fresh aromas of the earth, to feel the water while bathing, all these are ways of greeting.

I consider the trees, mountains and earth the same as people, only with a different form of life. But all have life. We shouldn't think that we are different. This tree is a living being. We, too, are living beings. The tree has been formed in its presentation. You have your form, your presentation. We have a way to communicate. The tree has its own form of communication.

It has a great life, a special characteristic of life — tranquility. There are many things you can learn from a tree.

I can learn many things from each of you if first I begin by saying hello to you. If I start by opening a channel of communication with you, if I open my heart, and I open my mind to you, then I can learn. But if I consider, or I think, that you are different and I don't say hello to you, I don't open my heart and my mind, I keep a distance from you, then I can't learn anything. And the same thing is true for the elements of nature.

The elements of nature are not only outside us. Exactly that which is outside, is also inside. We have a fire inside us. Is it possible? And how do we know that we have fire inside? The temperature of our body is a sign that something is on fire inside. We have water; we have air everywhere. We have air everywhere in our bodies. We have a sky. And our skin, our muscles, our bones are the stones, the desert. The respect towards nature also starts inside ourselves. When we greet and we respect, when we open our hearts and our minds, we start to learn incredible things.

We shouldn't think that the elements of nature are different from or inferior to us. There is one thing that unites us and makes us similar. They are alive like we are, just with a different presentation. It's only the external part that is different. Deep inside us and inside the elements of nature, there is the same spark of life.

So in our tradition we consider that to enter into contact with the elements of nature in a way that is born in the heart, with our mind as our friend, is very important. Can the mind be a friend with a waterfall? Can you sustain this? It's difficult if you think, but if you feel, it's easy.

The root cultures of our land, the people of those cultures, my culture, they have a daily habit. They have permanent contact with everything that is Life — an intimate contact with their own self,

an intimate contact with the things that you can touch — the plants, the earth, the water, the air — an intimate contact with the Father Sun. When I say contact, I don't mean to believe. It's about feeling. The mind might believe – I am a friend of the tree. But what the heart feels is, "I am the friend of the tree."

There are two different powers: mind and heart, Eagle and Condor. They need to fly together, these two birds, which are inside each one of us. It's necessary to think. It's necessary to feel.

The mind can tell us many things. "How can I talk with a tree?" It's a good question for the mind. The mind wants to hear the same sound that we use to communicate with each other. But the tree doesn't have the same organs that we have. It has other organs to communicate.

The heart of each one of us knows how to communicate. It can be by touching the tree, by looking, by hugging, by a feeling of respect, and through the channel of an open heart. And a message is going to arrive. Not to the mind, but to the heart. And then it passes on to the mind, and we will understand something that we weren't able to understand before, and our minds will say, "Oh yes – this is what I wanted to know!"

This time, that started in 1989, is perfectly suited to activate the power of the heart. It's the time adequate to feel more, more. We have enough information for the mind. Everybody that is here knows a lot of things, and the mind wants to know more, wants to read more, wants more technical knowledge, wants more spectacular things. But when you feel, you discover that what's simple has a great message.

To flow and to feel lets us advance on the personal path of our lives. When we think about our path, we get lost. When we feel the flow of our lives, then we advance. Where? Wherever we need to arrive. Where is that? Here. Here. Just here.

Inside each one of us, is everything. We only have to help ourselves to be more sensitive, to feel more. We have to give ourselves permission to be like children: spontaneous, natural. Many people, when

they see us feel and communicate with a tree, think we're crazy. It's necessary for us to make ourselves crazy — open to life.

It's necessary to fly in this time.

It's necessary to rise with the winds that are coming against us. When the circumstances are different from what we want, it's similar to a very strong wind that is coming against us. It is our opportunity. With that wind against us, we can fly higher. But a great majority of people do the opposite. When the circumstances are against them, they sink. It is necessary to open our hearts and our minds and to take advantage of the difficult circumstances of life, to understand the messages of life and to fly even higher.

It is necessary to bring out the wisdom that is inside you. The mind will say, "You are not wise." The mind will say, "You need to read more! Oh , you need to walk a lot further on the path still!" The mind is a great trainer. It's very useful. We have to chat with it. The mind is not our enemy. It's a

power of these times. It is better to be friendly with the mind.

But when it tells me that I still have a long way to go, or that I'm not wise yet, then I can tell it back, "I have everything I need for my life". I can tell the mind, "Now, I'm going to open the doors of my heart. I am going to start receiving the gifts of Life. I will feel life. I will discover all the marvelous things that life has given to me, that it has been giving to me since before I was born, and after I was born, too."

We have to feel, with the help of the wind, with the help of the water, with the help of the earth, with the help of the sacred fire, with the help of Father Sun, with the help of everything that life presents to us at each moment. When we feel this connection and this reality, then the things from the outside bother us less. The mind becomes calmer, and more friendly to us. It's there to train us, to try us, to strengthen us in our path.

4

Building Habits of Connecting

*To know things is very important. What's essential is
to live them and to practice them. It is better to know
just one or two things and to practice them. Now it is
time to dynamize and practice new habits — habits
of daily life, simple, sincere — so we can do them at
any moment, in any place.*

I INVITE YOU TO START creating new habits in your lives. These are habits of connecting, so we can connect our channels with the Great Spirit of Life, so we can cleanse the channels of communication. We need to open the channels of intimate friendship with all of Life.

In the human beings of early times, all the channels were open. Babies start with clean, open channels. Society and our way of living either help open or close these channels. The habits of life help open or close these channels.

It's necessary for us to create a culture of habits that help us clean and open these channels, a culture that leads us step by step to harmony. That's different from the way we live now. Our actions and activities must be filled with our heart. They must have a sense of meaning and transcendence. If we do just small simple things, it will open doors for us. To where? — to where we feel we must reach, to what we dream of reaching, to where we want to be, to that thing that we're looking for.

We need to remember that our habits have closed our channels. Certain social habits have cut that communication. So now it is time to 'dynamize' and practice new habits — habits of daily life, simple and sincere, so we can do them at any moment, in any place. Because it is not enough just to know. And the mind says, "We need to know  more." To know things is very important. But what's essential is to live them and to practice what we know. It is better to know just one or two things and to practice them. Every time we practice these habits with feeling, we can receive their gift to us.

One habit we can practice is greeting. When we greet each other, a channel of communication is opened. In this way, greet the day, the directions, everything. So then we are connected with Life itself always, in every place, in every moment. If I don't greet a person, that channel of communication does not open. Also, I cannot ask that person for anything if I haven't greeted them. This channel opens easily when our greeting is from the heart.

We can start with ourselves. Have we greeted ourselves? Our body is marvelous. We are not this body — the flesh, bones, blood. We are that something that gives life to this body. So we need to greet our body. In general, the mind thinks we are this body. We are not this body. The body is a great gift of Life in this reality. And that's why we need to feel our body; we need to be aware how we treat our body. How are the rivers in our body doing?

And it is the same with the elements. We must greet them if we wish to open a channel of communication with them. When we greet a plant, a stone, we're not greeting the physical but that which is within. When I greet a person, I don't greet their body. I greet what gives life to the physical presentation. Still, the physical presentation is very important because through

which is inner. Water and the other elements sustain life. There is a part of the Great Spirit of Life which is inside the water, and that is also in each one of us, and in air, water, fire, ushai, and in the six directions*. We're all different forms of expression of the Great Spirit of Life. Don't take this as a belief. It's a reality. A special force of the Great Spirit of Life is found in each direction. So to open the channels of communication, we need to greet the elements and the directions.

It's necessary that the elements of nature be as real for you as the people that you know, like your most intimate friends. We all have very close friends or family and with them we share a lot of things; we have a special connection with them. In the same way, we need to have that special connection with the elements of nature — to consid-

the physical presentation, I go to that which gives life.

We must greet the elements in the same way that we greet a person that we love. These elements are living beings. That water is not just chemical H_2O, not only a liquid, it's a part of the body of something. The water body is a physical representation of the essential

* N, S, E, W, to the cosmos (above), and to Mother Earth (below).

er them like we consider our closest friends and family. If we have the belief that the elements are different than close friends and family, we won't have that closeness. Only their physical appearance is different. But the essence, the spirit, the

 essential characteristic is the same as for any one of us. Our body has this presentation. The physical presentation of the elements is how they are – their bodies. But within this body, within the bodies of the elements, is the essence of Life. Everything is alive. Everything has consciousness.

My intention is to remove those boundaries of culture, so we consider ourselves to be more part of Mother Nature. So that we really feel we are children of Mother Nature. So that we feel that the life that beats out there is also inside of us. So that we realize the truth that the quality of life depends on the quality of the elements. So that we go back to truth, not to the fantasy that we are separate.

Ushai is the word we use in Kichwa to refer to the unity, the oneness, the power of the four elements in equilibrium, in balance. When you don't feel the elements are different from you, when you feel you are earth, fire, wind, water, and that everything is the Great Spirit of Life, then there is no difference. It's necessary to get there. The obstacle is the mind.

So let's remember to be close to an element, like we are close to friends or family. As with people, at the beginning, we're not immediately intimate. We need to meet

several times, have sincere expressions. It's necessary to greet each other, to express our feeling. It's necessary to search to understand their presence, to listen to them, to speak with them, to give them gifts.

Everything you want to express, express to an element. Become intimate friends. Just do as you would with someone you want to become close with, someone you consider very special, with whom you're interested in getting close. Express everything and then, when we become friends, we continue expressing, so we become not just friends, but more than friends.

Slowly, step by step, we need to get rid of the cultural lies about the elements.

I remember when I was young, I tried to get good grades. In public school they taught that water is inert, without flavor or odor. I couldn't accept that because my parents taught that water is the origin of Life. And I have visited a lot of streams. Every one has a special flavor, color, sound, odor, a particular life. What I was taught in school was a total lie. So the day of the exam, I answered, I put what I knew and I got a zero. The teacher said, "Why didn't you comprehend that water is flavorless, colorless, etc.?" "Because I have experienced it," I said. The teacher said, "You have another chance," but I put the same answer. I wanted a good grade, but I got a zero.

It is necessary to act in truth and with what we feel. If someone approaches us with sincerity, we open up. We easily give our friendship to them and if we have common interests with them, we can become more than friends. That is why I want to explain how to become intimate with the elements in nature.

Do you like the idea of expressing something from the heart to one of the elements – whatever you feel, an expression, to a person or being with whom you want to have a relationship? So we can think, "How can I express that feeling to an element?" First choose an element. What is the gift, the sound, my expression to this element?

In the Andes, when we go to a stream, we bring food and wine to express gratitude. When we get there, we leave the gifts. We say and feel beautiful things for the river, or for the mountain. We spend some time, sharing the food; we talk, listen, receive its gift. We give thanks, we say goodbye and go back — in the same way as when we go to visit a family member or friend. People

believe we're worshipping. We are simply expressing our friendship. Sometimes we bring music and we dance. So there are many ways to express this happiness and friendship. Anthropologists refer to these as 'payments'. Researchers refer to these as 'rituals'. For me, Life itself is a permanent ritual. Every place and every moment is sacred. In Kichwa there is no word for sacred or not sacred. We feel from the smallest to the greatest, everything is sacred.

By doing these greetings and expressions continuously, it helps us clean and open our channels. This is an action made with our heart, with feeling. Some practices done without feeling, become mechanical. The practices have great power if we feel them. The same practice done mechanically won't help or have the same results. For this reason we need to start being more spontaneous, more creative. Spirituality and creativity are qualities of the heart. Technique and accuracy, are related to the mind. We are not trying to fight against the mind. Both mind and the heart are essential — to think and to feel, to feel and to think, eagle and condor, flying together in harmony and clarity within us.

Another habit that helps clean and open our channels is to give thanks for the gifts we've received. We must express our gratitude — in every place, every time we breathe, every time we eat earth transformed into food, every time can see, can speak, can listen, can feel our touch, can walk, for everything, for every gift — be very thankful. If we express gratitude, we begin to open a channel of communication with the elements.

Another habit we can practice, just before going to sleep, is to give thanks for the day and for the opportunity to learn while dreaming. For me, the waking hours are the day of the sun; going to sleep is the day of the moon. Also at sunset, give thanks for the day of the sun and greet the day of the moon. That is a beginning. The form, the way, the time you do it, is personal,

from the spontaneity and creativity of each person. The essential thing is not to do it mechanically or by obligation. We should do it as we feel it from within our heart, feeling what we're doing.

I know spiritual people who work with the elements but forget to give gratitude. People want to get more. When we greet the elements, we give gratitude also. Not giving thanks is like wanting to go into the room where there is wisdom but not being willing to open the

door. Our life should be a permanent expression of gratitude. Step by step we will reach there.

In order to expand and start to wake up our consciousness, it's necessary to feel. When we start feeling, we're going to start to have clarity about these practices and about living wisely. If we feel, this is another habit to help us clean and open the channels. Then we will not waste the gifts of Nature.

For example, we need to take only the amount of food we'll use. How can we connect with Mother Earth if we throw away her gift? It is not enough to say a prayer before

our meal, and then waste the food. There's abundance of food here. You should be very grateful, because you were born in circumstances where food is abundant. Express gratitude. Use it wisely. Possibly in the same moment when you have abundant food, in another place, there is not enough. It's necessary to practice fasts. It helps clean the body and helps you to value food. In other places, there are people fasting because they don't have food. When those people find even a little food, they feel very grateful and don't waste any of it. I give thanks to Mother Earth because I've had the experience of this. Possibly my habit of eating is not political. For me, it's not possible to waste any food, because I feel it is the love from Mother Earth. I have an intimate connection with Mother Earth. I receive infinite gifts from Mother Earth. And the least I can do is not waste it.

Having abundance is a blessing. And it can transform into the opposite when you don't use it correctly. But also poverty is a blessing for it helps us feel immensely when we receive just a simple thing – to feel very grateful. In the Andes, you can see small children running barefoot, but their eyes are glowing with happiness.

Every person was born in the circumstances they needed. We need to be grateful for those circumstances and use them correctly. Material poverty can also turn from a blessing to a danger.

So material things are a complement, not the essential. People who don't have material things think that when they do they'll be happy. The ones who have a lot are bored. They want something simple.

The essential thing is to feel gratitude for what we have and use it in the best way possible. We should feel grateful and give gratitude for what we have and take advantage of what we have. And one way to take advantage is to give gratitude, to be grateful for your circumstances.

The true teacher is waiting within us. It manifests in daily life when our actions are directed to harmony. We are, little by little, becoming loving children of Mother Nature. Most people are ungrateful children of Mother Nature. Some may say, "I love Mother Nature," but their actions tell a different story.

We need to be consistent with what we say and what we do, in a simple and sincere way. We need to apply the things we already know. With what we already know, with what we have learned already, we need to take an inventory of what we do, of how much of what we know we actually practice. Then we won't want to know more. And our mind will be more tranquil. The mind tends to tell us that we need to know more.

The invitation is to act and live according to our dreams, according to what we truly want. I'm not saying that knowing more is bad. Knowing more brings more responsibility. It is worse to do something when you know you're not supposed to do it.

So the simple habits are very important in our path. It is important to practice what we already know. Many things, techniques, philosophies we already know. Now we need to select them and practice – practice whatever you're drawn to.

I'm not talking about extraordinary things, but simple things from daily life. The invitation is to experiment with things you already know, in daily life. We can use simple practices that help us feel more, reflections that help us comprehend the great within the simple. Through these practices and reflections — by greeting the elements, by giving thanks, by feeling the preciousness of life and not wasting, by feeling and becoming intimate with the elements, by expressing our feeling, our love to them— we can feel the sacredness of life, in every moment, in every place. Then we are filled with happiness. Then we are truly nourished.

5

Connecting with Earth

Every time we eat, it's a great opportunity to connect with Earth. In reality what we eat is earth transformed with the help of the elements of nature. It is the love of Mother Earth crystallized, the immense love of Mother Earth.

To feel the food we eat is to feel the power of Mother Earth.

MOTHER EARTH gives us many lessons. For example, she is always giving. And she transforms negativity into the sublime. Another lesson of Mother Earth is sharing. She's always sharing her gifts. We should learn from that and be able to share. Mother Earth is a union of life – of all aspects. Remember, we have a body that is earth. All things around us are earth – the computer, the car are earth. Clothes are earth; food is earth. So we have a lot of opportunities for connecting with earth.

We can enter into the secrets of Mother Nature, and we can be sons and daughters, apprentices to the wisdom of the Mother Earth. What's the channel of wisdom of Mother Nature? It's food. Everything we eat is earth — earth transformed with the immense love of our Mother. That love has made it possible that from compost, comes a fruit with a delicious odor, with a very attractive look to us, with colors that are very appealing to us, and delicious and varied tastes for our appetite. That's what the love of Mother Nature does.

Let's not forget that each meal is a great opportunity. It's a great opportunity to put ourselves in intimate contact with the love of Mother Earth. When we put ourselves in contact with the love of Mother Earth, we receive her secrets, her love. In the moment that we're eating something physical, we're actually bringing the love into our hearts. We're eating the love, giving nutrition to our hearts. We can realize that everything we eat is love from Mother Nature. Every moment we nourish our body, let's nourish our hearts as well. Let's not only fill our stomachs, but our hearts as well. If you're eating mechanically, you only fill your stomach. If you eat with joy and gratitude, you fill your stomach and you fill your heart. That's how we should all do it — to fill our hearts, and fill our lives, in every moment of our lives.

Food has made a great journey to arrive to us – miracle after miracle – with smells, flavors, colors, forms. Everything has been dedicated to us. It is a gift of the Great Pachamama, Mother Nature, and the Great Spirit of Life. We are their children. They love us so much, their children, that they give us these gifts. It's a great shame to eat without feeling. Every time we're aware of these miracles of how the wheat and tomato came – who grew them, who transported them, who packed them, who prepared them, what dreams they had, and how they arrived here with us, how we feel them in our mouths — then we are truly nourished.

There are two things — spirit and matter. When we're aware of the miracles of how our food came to be, it's going to fill us physically and spiritually. If we're aware of these miracles, gratitude emerges spontaneously, and gratitude brings happiness. We become full of light, full of Life, full of wisdom. Gratitude is an expression that brings so many gifts. We can practice this simply three times per day. And some eat more frequently!

The doorway that opens to wisdom is eating with gratitude. If you forget, when you remember, practice again. This is the most real and permanent religion. It's spirituality without saying 'I'm spiritual'. It's so simple. Heaven is not far away. It's here. The doorway to wisdom is not far away. It's closer than we think.

For the mind, it's difficult. If you think 'How am I going to do it? ", you can't do it. But if you go towards the grapes, and you go with gratitude, and more gratitude for the taste in your mouth, more gratitude because they have vita-

mins that help your body, and more gratitude because they give pleasure to your taste, and then you can feel more and more gratitude for what you feel — then it's easy. Don't think too much! Do it!

It's necessary when eating to feel joy – to enjoy is a way of thanking for the gifts of the elements of nature. It's a way to give thanks for the gift of food. In food, there are all the elements together. The harmony of those elements produces the fifth element – the ushai. When we are connected with these gifts, these gifts have a very special energy. Therefore, we're going to eat the energy that fills our heart and our spirit. We should never eat just to fill the stomach. We need to eat to fill the heart, the spirit and also the stomach. Buen provecho!

Give thanks before eating and give thanks after. If you have something to express, express it! Then you can simply enjoy eating with gratitude. How we regard the food gives it energy.

When we feel gratitude to Mother Nature, every portion of food is a great gift. This gratitude does not allow us to waste. We feel it is a special gift from our Mother. Every bit of food will be something really special and this connection with the food will be the best prayer to the earth. Through this we'll connect to all the elements in a natural way. We'll have gratitude toward water, the water within food, toward the

sun and the moon, which made it grow, toward the people who grew the food.

One moment of connection, and life is transformed. All the non-happy things in our lives vanish in that moment. If we're able to extend, to 'grow' this moment of connection to the other moments of our lives, sadness will mostly be gone.

The sun, and wind are nourishment as well. In reality food is everything and everywhere. Air is food; sunlight is food; different smells are food; seeing each other is food; touching is food; listening, talking, dancing singing, everything in life is food. When the word food comes up, the mind thinks, "Only for the stomach."

There are many foods we receive through the eyes. The gorgeous brilliant green of plants in spring is a special food. To laugh is a special food. According to the concept we have of food, that's how we are fed. If we ingest laughter, then we're feeding the heart. All activities that spontaneously come from our heart are a special meal.

6

Connecting with Air

Do you think it's important to have gratitude toward the breath, to feel with our heart, gratitude toward the air that we breathe? It's the channel for communication with the power of the air.

WE ARE ALWAYS BREATHING. We can take advantage of this every moment. Feel how the breath comes in through the nose, circulates through the head, and in our throats. Feel it fill up our lungs. Let yourself enjoy the possibility of life that air brings for us.

We can receive great benefit by feeling our breathing in each moment. Breathing is something that we do, in every moment, in every place. We breathe. If, in this moment, you try to breathe with feeling, it will be different than what you were doing with no feeling. If we feel our breathing in, as we fill our lungs, we will also fill our hearts. We should use every circumstance in our life, and every moment, to fill our hearts, and to fill our lives.

We can take advantage in the moment we breathe — in every moment — by giving thanks for each breath. As we breathe in, we can give thanks that this air is sustaining our lives. And step by step we'll be discovering that all the activities of our lives are miraculous, and we'll be able to enjoy every moment of life.

Shall we practice? It's simple; it's easy. In a natural way, you take the breath in at your own rhythm, and you fill yourself however much you want, and fill yourself with everything that you want. When you're full, wait a moment. Don't let go. And then let the air out with your mouth, very softly, but do it with feeling. If you do it mechanically, you won't take advantage of this exercise. To breathe feeling gratitude, because it's Life that we're receiving — this is the experience we can practice.

And we can continue doing this practice, being conscious of  the fact that we are receiving Life. And we do it with gratitude, in every place, at every moment that we're aware of this, because ever since we were born, we've been breathing all the time. Now the only difference is to do it feeling gratitude, no matter what we're doing. If we're walking, we're breathing with gratitude. If we're cooking, we're also breathing with gratitude. If you're driving, also, breathing with gratitude. If you're on the phone, breathing with gratitude. On the computer, breathe with gratitude. Is it possible?

Now let's close our eyes and breathe slowly — feeling our breathing. But remember, this practice we can also do constantly, without closing our eyes. We're always breathing – we have the opportunity every time, to feel our breathing. In every time, in every place, we have the opportunity to feel the air. It's natural for the mind to tell us that we need to go to a place and meditate. My invitation is – we can do this at every time, in every place. We need this benefit at every moment. This can become a habit. We'll discover beautiful things. Then we'll not only know about air, we'll discover the power of air — it's Life.

Practice this little by little. If you forget, it doesn't matter! Start again. Do you think it's important to have gratitude to the breath, to feel with your heart, gratitude to the air that we breathe? It's the channel for communication to the

power of the air. It's simple. It's natural. I'm not a friend of complicated techniques and methods and for this we don't need an official school where we have to read lots of books, or memorize things that in life we will never use.

Are you still feeling your breathing? It's not important if you forget. What's important is that each time you remember, you do it, so you get into the custom, the habit of this. Each time you remember, continue to put it into practice. Remember not to do this as some very serious thing. It should be like a children's game. Children will play a game, and maybe they can't do it well, but they will repeat the game. It's important to find happiness as you practice this. If you practice very seriously, maybe you'll do the physical part, but not reach the essence of it.

You can also practice feeling the air in another way. If a person

feels the air around their body, it's like a fish being in water. We're inside air. It's like we're inside a big fish bowl of air!

One help to feeling the air is through the flight of a bird or when we hold a feather and rub along it, you can feel the quality of air. And we can hear the power of the air, of the wind, blowing through the forest, breathing with the movement of the tree tops. We can see it in the dancing leaves. I like to lie down and see how the wind moves the leaves. I transport myself more rapidly if clouds are in the sky. If clouds or trees move with the wind one way, it feels as if you are moving in the opposite direction. Ever try it?

7

Connecting with Water

*Who does not love being close to a body of
water, a river, a lake, a pond, or the ocean?
The water has a natural attraction for us.
We can benefit just by sitting near such a
body of water. Its qualities fascinate us.*

I HAVE ONE SIMPLE RECOMMENDA-TION for feeling the power of water: take advantage of your shower in the morning. We can do this simply by feeling the water on our skin, by feeling its caress. We can use the shower and caress the water softly with the palms of our hands, feeling  it circulate in the space between our fingernails. As you do this, express what your heart wishes.

The most marvelous things are quite simple, when you begin to feel. Often we are looking for sophisticated practices and fancy ceremonies. The mind likes to search for these things, and there is no end to the search. What we need is practice, and we can practice with what we already have or do right now.

Using feeling transforms the most common actions into ceremonies, making them marvelous and magical acts.

There are many other ways to use the power of water, and you do not need fancy rituals to do it. To feel water we can go to a river or a pond. We can also take advantage of rain. Feel the rain!

The Eagle with its books says we are at least 50% water, and some cells are more than 75% water, so we can use that information to transform this water into a ceremony of feeling. So let us feel the water that runs through our own veins, because the mind can tell you, you who live in busy cities, that you don't have time to go to the river. If time is short,

It's important to practice relating to water. Just like with people, on meeting for the first time, one is a little careful. Then you start talking more, then greet and little by little become friends. Sincerity and common interests are necessary. With time and openness of the heart, the relationship becomes more intimate. Time and your heart will help you become friends with the elements of nature. When you become intimate friends, just like with people, if you need something, the friend is ready to help.

your body is sufficient, for you can feel the water within you, right where you are, right now.

Water is a being with a body and spirit. Everything expresses, speaks to us and listens. Water is very sensitive. Water transforms. Water reacts in different ways. When we give love to water, water cleanses us; water gives us tranquility; water heals us — when we give love with our mind and heart. Speaking only from our mind, water doesn't respond.

With water, there are different moments of approach — when taking a shower, when drinking, using water, connecting with the water inside the body, and with our blood – the inner rivers. Intimate relationship with water is not just outside, but inside also.

To be close to water is easy because our body is mostly water, and our food is also. In each moment, every place, we have the opportunity to be friends with water. If we have the opportunity to go to a waterfall or river, we also have the opportunity to see water. There are many ways and opportunities for us to be friends with water. It's important to practice in every moment, in every place. Then the mind will bother you less and less.

Water reacts according to how we act toward water. The water that is outside responds to our feeling. If we feel love for water, the water will respond in the same way towards us, with more love.

For me, one way to help decontaminate water is for us to think and feel that water is clean and pure. Then, water at the molecular level starts to regenerate itself. But if we think water is contaminated, we contaminate it more.

Remember we're more than 50% water. Just as in the way that if we tell someone, "You're ugly; you're dumb," they become worse, or sick; instead we can think they're getting better and better, and help them. The body will react to what the people around think and feel

– since the body is largely water. The water has a great power of accumulating information. All of nature has a great amount of water in it. In the air, there's water; even in fire, you have water.

We're going to take a walk with water. Listen to the sound of water. Allow ourselves to express, each one of us, what we feel listen-ing to the sound of water. Look for connection with water. When you feel a connection, let your heart feel whatever it feels. This practice can be however you feel it. The mind thinks that it's easier close to a river or waterfall. "I'll wait until I'm near water." Remember, your body has a high percentage of water.

Every day, feel water. When taking a shower, when drinking water. We need to get past the limi-tations that the mind will place. Each person has a different form of connecting with water. You can have intimate contact with water anytime your heart wants. And it's very healthy. Water cleanses not only skin. It also cleanses certain things that don't allow us to walk or continue in freedom.

When water flows and there's any obstruction, the water doesn't go back, it continues to look for another path. Maybe it will find a little space and that will give it a very large power; in many cases it will continue with more force. We need to learn this from water. If we have difficult circumstances in our life, we can remember how water won't go back. It will look for the exit. It will rise into a space and look for the exit with harmony, softly. It can be slow or fast, but naturally it will proceed.

This intimate contact with water can give us everything we want in our lives – materially and spiritually. I believe that in different cultures and philosophies and mystical traditions, water always has a great place. In modern life, people are separated from this respect for water. We who want a life of harmony and plenty, need to act in a natural way with water.

Let's practice in every moment and every place – this spontaneous and natural relationship of love and gratitude with water.

8

Connecting with Fire

*Each of us has Sacred Fire ignited within ourselves,
within our bodies. This Sacred Fire illuminates our
life. The Sacred Fire makes the colors come alive.
This Sacred Fire makes us see in something very
simple, something sacred.*

To FEEL FIRE ITSELF we can do various ceremonies or simple rituals. We can light a fire, a candle, we can burn some incense. Look at a flame for a moment. Then close your eyes, but keep on seeing it. Repeat this. Search to feel the heat inside, the light inside.

Fire, the same as the other elements, is essential for life. We have it ignited inside our bodies – each one of us. We can tap into the fire inside us through feeling the heat of our body and through passions, through emotions. Fire burns destructive things in the body. It gives light. Friendship and love help us feel sacred fire. Here you have the sweat lodge. In Ecuador we have a wide variety of natural hot springs. Fire is also naturally therapeutic. You can throw symbolically into a fire that which is troubling you, that which you no longer need. We can use interior or exterior resources to feel the power of fire.

Many times the mind may think that in order to create a sacred fire, we need a great open space to make a bonfire. That's an external fire. But each of us has sacred fire ignited within ourselves, within our bodies. In many root cultures, they speak about sacred fire. In my language, Kichwa, the word, "sex" doesn't exist. The understanding is different. Everything to do with sexual matters is called sacred fire. The sacred fire represents that part which helps to activate life. The sacred fire transforms many things.

In an external fire, the circle of stones is the feminine sexual organ – that's why we get close to the fire with respect. The wood represents the masculine aspect.

The union of the two together produces the activation of life. Fire constantly activates, keeps bringing life to life. Another manifestation of sacred fire is that love we feel that we can't put into words.

This sacred fire illuminates our life. The sacred fire makes the colors come alive. This sacred fire makes us see in something very simple – something sacred. The sacred fire is very powerful. If someone uses it without respect, they can get burned. Because of sacred fire, we are all embodied. It permits life to continue. Sacred fire allows transformation from one state to another.

With sacred fire, one can illuminate life – or one can have the same faith as moths do when they fly into fire. Let's remember we're not insects. We need to be illuminated by fire, not burned by it, and be able to feel the warmth, but

not so much as to get burned. We need to keep sacred fire, but not let it spread to burn other things. Sacred fire is not to terminate or end, but to illuminate constantly. Sacred fire is meant to transform us constantly.

We need to reflect on this issue of the sacred fire inside each of us. Remember in our minds what concepts we might have so we can honor the fire. The sacred fire is not just the union of two people. The sacred fire is also when two hearts feel something special.

Everything in nature gets activated through the sacred fire. Nothing in nature exists without the sacred fire. The flowers are the sexual organs of the plants and they are where you find the most beautiful colors and fragrances and they always face toward the sun. When sacred fire happens in a flower, the fruit comes out and that fruit contains the sacred fire of the plant – with a tree, too. A tree is a sacred fire that is materialized.

Each of us has sacred fire inside us, and thanks to that sacred fire, we can perceive the light. Thanks to that sacred fire, we can understand and transform. The sacred fire gives new life and it also helps

transform things we don't need to carry with us.

In this time, it is the time of women, and women are the ones that can better utilize sacred fire. I've seen in many cities how the statue of liberty is a woman with a torch. Now it is the time of women with sacred fire, illuminating the path.

9

Letting Go of Baggage, Receiving Gifts

*Many people at this time need to have their
own special gift, but they can't receive it.
They allow it to be lost, because they're filled
with things they don't need.*

Letting Go of Baggage

MANY PEOPLE ARE TRAVELING with a lot of baggage that is totally unnecessary. But the mind thinks we should carry that load. In this path we are going to climb mountains, so we need to get rid of our baggage.

We should also be ready to let go of the things we shouldn't carry anymore. We shouldn't keep our pain, our worry, our suffering. Whatever bothers you – begin to let go of it. The things we should let go of – they're not bad. They're simply not for this time in our lives. We're thankful they've come to us. Now we say goodbye and we allow them to go away. When you let go of something that bothers you – you can receive something you need.

Many times we're suffering because we don't understand certain circumstances, or we don't want to understand certain circumstances. Many people are with their suffering that's pushing them down, and they don't want to let go of it. The different elements of nature, like the air, the fire, and the earth and the water, we can use them so that these difficult things are taken away by the elements.

There are many difficulties and illnesses that water can help us with. Other things the wind can take away. Others, Mother Earth can transform. Other difficulties, other illnesses, the sacred fire can transform. Everything that exists in nature is a gift for us that we

doesn't allow us to let go of things.

It's also very helpful to make good use of the elements. For example, the wind. The power of the wind can be very therapeutic, helping cleanse the mind of thoughts it no longer needs, and that you are ready to let go of. Wind can carry them away leaving the mind empty, leaving you relaxed and free. Try it when your mind seems cluttered or you are burdened with disturbing thoughts. Go outside and give them to the wind. Let the wind sweep your mind clean. The wind can take away many things that are in our soul and give us things that are very necessary for us. When we feel the air, we have the possibility of letting go the things we don't want and we also have the great possibility of receiving the gifts we all deserve.

can take advantage of, but let's not use them to hurt ourselves. A fruit in excess can hurt us, if we eat too much of it. But if we eat it with love, in a natural way, it can greatly benefit us.

There are various ways we can let go. For example – to laugh. It helps us let go. Being too serious

Our mind knows many things and it knows the power of water

for cleansing our skin. But we can now add to this the power of feeling with attention to cleanse the inside as well. We can do this simply by feeling the water on our skin, feeling its caress. We can feel its power entering our pores, and if we can feel that this water not only cleanses our skin, but purifies us within as well, then we will enjoy more benefit from our bathing. This is bathing with feeling, which makes it a sacred ceremony of inner and outer cleansing where we let go of things we no longer need. As with eating mechanically when we only feed the body and fail to feel the love of Mother Earth, so with bathing. If we do it mechanically, without feeling and awareness, we only cleanse the skin and our insides remain unaffected. But when we do it with feeling, our insides can benefit as well.

In difficult circumstances we can use the lesson of water to flow. Water can be stuck, but it's always looking to continue flowing. The

great majority of people don't want to apply the lesson of water when they're stuck. The invitation from life is to take from this lesson of water. The same goes for the toilet, we can eliminate physical and emotional and spiritual impurities at the same time, letting go of baggage we no longer want or need, making room for new gifts.

Fire is also naturally therapeutic. You can use it to get rid of emotional patterns and painful

memories that are troubling you, or that you no longer need to feed. You can throw them symbolically in the fire and let its power burn them away. But this won't work if you don't feel the fire burning away these things. It won't work mechanically. You must feel the fire burning up the things you no longer need.

Mother Earth transforms negativity into the sublime. One can lie on the earth, or even be buried in earth (with the head free!) to release negativity or trauma. Feeling ourselves in our Mother's embrace, feeling her love for us, helps us release what we need to.

If we don't clean our house, it's not easy to receive more things. Our house has many rooms. The big room is the mind. There are many things we don't need in our

mind. We have many anxieties and worries and we can discard them. Another beautiful room is the heart. It can be full of things we shouldn't keep. We should clear the room of our heart and the elements can help us. We have rooms filled with memories — of sadness and suffering. We should clean them. We also have many images, photos of ourselves. We think we are this way, but we want another form. We should not keep these images that are not real.

When you're free and your house is free of many things you shouldn't have, your house has more space for new gifts that are meant for you at this time. None of us want these gifts to stay outside in the rain because there's no space — but this happens. Many people at this time need to have their own special gift, but they can't receive

it. They allow it to be lost, because they're filled with things they don't need.

Receiving Gifts

TO BE ABLE TO RECEIVE OUR GIFTS, it's important to feel the elements of Nature. We can feel air, fire, earth, and water. Each one of us should practice with the element that we identify with. Every person is identified with one or two elements. We should start to feel with the element we identify ourselves with. We should remember not to do this too seriously. Children connect quickly with the elements of nature. Many children live permanently in contact with the elements because they're not serious – they're playing.

In reality, all the things in life that we have are opportunities to play. What happens is – older people have ingrained in our mind that things are serious and the mind has believed this – that we have to be serious. It's good that we look at ourselves in the mirror when we're serious. The mirror will help us see we shouldn't have that face! Animals can also help us to feel the elements of Nature.

We've understood that this quality of feeling is very important in our lives. This quality of feeling helps your life. Your life fills. Colors become brighter. Eyes are brighter. Our lives have meaning. If we can feel, life is continuous. Gifts are in every place, in every moment. In an encounter, I discover what I need, because I don't have words of wanting, not wanting, needing, not needing. When you feel, everything is exact. It's not like the mind

thinks it is. It's how it is. And then gratitude arises spontaneously.

It is natural, after receiving so many gifts – to feel gratitude. From the heart, to return something is a natural reaction. The cosmos is in a permanent equilibrium. When we receive gifts, we should return gifts in different forms and circumstances. What's important is that they come from the heart. Mother Nature gives – and we feel gratitude. As an analogy, when we get a loan from the bank, we return it with some interest. It is the same with relationships among people. The heart experiences joy when it receives and when it gives, and then it has the right to receive more.

To feel joy is a way of expressing gratitude to life. Sometimes you force yourself, thinking to give thanks with the mind, but it doesn't flow. But the joy a person feels naturally — that's a way of giving thanks. To live in a happy way is a way of bringing gratitude to life. Then inside ourselves we feel very rich.

The invitation is to make every day of our life a party, a fiesta. This does not depend on the calendar, but on each of us. We don't need a governmental decree. Just wake up and tell our mind, "This is another day to celebrate!" The mind will say, "What are we going to celebrate?" There are so many things we can celebrate every day – the new day, that we can see, feel, walk, learn. The common can become special, even driving a car! This is a way of being able to do well with abundance. My invitation is that every day be a celebration.

In my experience there are no beings that don't have gratitude. People express it differently. Appreciating the dawn, feeling thirst, drinking and feeling refreshed, two people loving each other, friends talking and laughing — all are forms of gratitude. In reality everyone lives with gratitude. Our mind might have a different concept of how to express gratitude. It is more beautiful if the mind can enter too, into the expression of gratitude along with every part of our body — speaking, eating, breathing, cooking. There's gratitude in crying, sleeping, resting. All moments are great opportunities for gratitude. To exist is a great gift.

In other philosophies they speak of ecstasies, of samadhi. It's this feeling of total joy, of plenitude. This feeling of joy — learn how to prolong it more and more.

In Kichwa, we call it "sumak kausay" — full complete life. The feeling — I could die now and it would be fine!

In the same way that the expression of gratitude happens when we feel things, likewise emerges love. And you feel love towards yourself and a lot of love towards the people your eyes can see and the people your eyes cannot see. When we experience this feeling of gratitude and love, this is happiness. Happiness is not an objective where I will go. Happiness is a continuous expression of ourselves — the feeling from the inside, and the receiving from the outside.

This feeling can be expressed through words, through the eyes, in every action. Through words I can say, "I love you." It's not a formality; it's a feeling. That's happiness. Happiness is not far away. Happiness is not impos-

sible to reach. It's not our objective. Happiness IS. Happiness IS. To breathe is happiness. To walk, to see, to listen, to talk, is happiness. When we feel these everyday things, we're filled with light, with happiness.

Where are our problems? Where are the difficulties? If there are difficult circumstances, with this way of feeling, the difficult circumstance is a great opportunity. To the difficulty we can also say, "Thank you." It's an opportunity to fly higher, to feel more, to express more clearly — love.

When we are able to feel, we should not let go of that feeling. We should keep it with us and make it bigger. To feel every time, more. Every moment is another opportunity to feel more, with ourselves and with others. If I am filled with light, happiness, love, if you are filled with light, happiness, love, you are going to radiate. You will not be thinking about helping or wanting to help others. You'll radiate. You'll be full of light, happiness, and love. We should fill ourselves in every time, in every place with this. The things that are contrary to this — we should take them out of our lives.

10

Every Moment, Every Place is an Opportunity

*When I was young, a grandmother told me
— not one circumstance in life is negative.
It might be very difficult, but when we've
passed it, we're left with learning.*

IN EVERY PLACE AND EVERY MOMENT, we have great opportunities. Let's not think that we have certain places, and that those places alone are places where we can fill ourselves and feel special, and that those places are special. The whole world is special. Let's not think that there are only certain moments that we can feel special things. Every moment, every place is special, and we can receive special things.

We can wake up, and see the new day, and fill ourselves with happiness. And each moment of the day, we can take advantage of this, to fill ourselves. And when we lay down in bed, we can appreciate the entire day and also we can appreciate the opportunity to lie down and rest, and that our dreams should be lessons of our life, our path. When we leave our body in the bed, we have an opportunity to learn lots of things that here on earth we are not able to learn.

We are one with Mother Nature. We receive the benefits of Mother Nature. The problems of life are natural. This connection with Mother Nature helps us to feel better with our problems. Equally, diseases are a form of disequilibrium. When we connect with the elements of nature, we become happier, and we find solutions to the problems and the sickness. Therefore, we should think and feel that nature is with us. We should think and feel that with nature, we are one.

And this connection we can feel anywhere, and at any time. Remember that everything we face is an opportunity to walk our path. When we eat, an opportunity to increase our intimacy with Mother Earth is given to us. Every time we breathe, an opportunity for an intimate relationship with air is given us. When we feel the warmth in our bodies, when we feel friendship and love, this is a channel of communication with the sacred fire. To drink water, to wash ourselves, is a great opportunity to clean the physical part as well as those other aspects that need to be cleaned. In this way, our life becomes transparent and fluid.

Birds don't fight the wind. They use it to elevate themselves. Trees make sounds with the strong winds. There are many possibilities to convert moments of blockage or difficulty. These problems can help us walk through our life more carefully with more knowledge and awareness. When I was young, a grandmother told me – Not one circumstance in life is negative. It might be very difficult, but when we've passed it, we're left with learning.

The great majority of people don't remember God when things are going well. My invitation to you is that we remember the Great Spirit in all moments, all days. One of the ways to remember the Great Spirit is with gratitude. Gratitude is a way we can notice the Great Force of Life.

All of us have difficult moments in life. In those moments, it's natural that one can feel, "What can I feel grateful for?" I'm not going to tell you the difficult things of my life, but all indigenous people pass and continue to pass through many difficult things, and so did I, until I understood what my grandmother told me. Not only when it's sunny, should you give gratitude. You have to give gratitude when the clouds are dark and the rain is falling. I thought she was talking about the sun and the rain and the natural phenomenon. But I realized that what my grandmother was saying had a lot more teaching in it.

When I lived very difficult moments, and I started to feel gratitude for that difficult moment, my mind would say, "But you're crazy! How can you grateful for this difficult moment?" But my grandmother's words took more power in me, and I gave even more thanks for that difficult moment. I couldn't see the end of that difficulty, and my mind said, "That's the way you're going to be until you die." And I continued to say, "Thank you," until one moment, without me doing anything, because I couldn't do anything, years passed, and things began to change slowly.

Maybe your difficulties are larger than mine. Maybe you need wiser things that are inside you. But it is something else that I'm saying now. I'm saying now, that when the winds blow very strong against us, when difficulties are very strong against us, we can fly higher. That's what I learned from the condor. The condor waits until there's a strong wind against him, because he's the largest bird in the world, and when there's a strong wind against him, he throws himself in the void and flies higher.

And when the difficulties are coming towards us, we have even greater possibilities of discovering wisdom inside us. I don't call the difficulties! Difficulties just come on their own! And I remember what my grandparents told me, and I start giving gratitude with all my heart, and I throw myself. And now I've flown high.

We can feel and give gratitude for these gifts — in every situation, in every moment. Then, we put ourselves in harmony with life. And the problems become less and less, dissolving. Many times the problems are our teachers. It's very simple, very simple. We shouldn't close ourselves to receiving the gifts of life. We should have our minds and hearts open to receive.

Every element, every thing, exists in this reality to help us get rid of what we need to get rid of and to receive those gifts that we need to receive. For this reason, every moment and in every circumstance is an opportunity. When one achieves this connection with the elements then respect and gratitude arise naturally. One doesn't need to think of being grateful. It comes naturally. We become aware that we depend on the elements and that we are part of the Great Force of Life, and the Great Force of Life is part of us as well.

11

Kuyanimi — I love you

*Through the connection with the elements
we can perceive the Creator of Life. We can
say, "I feel God."*

MANY CULTURES IN THE WORLD have their lives directed in the way of feeling. Others, especially modern cultures, have their lives directed to thinking. In this time, it is necessary to have an equilibrium, a balance. Societies focused only on thinking, should cultivate feeling. Cultures that have been only feeling, should cultivate thinking. Both powers – to think and to feel – are important in this time. When a person is focused only in one direction, there are empty places in his or her life. The easiest way to balance ourselves is by being in contact with the different elements of Nature. It is through the elements that we have a direct channel to the Great Spirit of Life.

Always remember that we are not outside of Mother Nature. We are part of the Great Mother Nature. We shouldn't forget that we are within the Great Spirit of Life. We're part of the Great Spirit of Life. The mind has lied to us, has tricked us. And it has convinced people that they are apart from nature, separated from the Great Spirit of Life. But in truth, we are part of Mother Nature and we're part of the Great Spirit of Life. To stop feeling this truth results in confusion and suffering. Many people in society now are confused, are suffering.

Each person has a key – it could be the breath, or to listen to water. And you can activate your key doing whatever you're drawn to. A person can have various keys, not just one. One only needs to activate the key. The mechanism to activate is to feel. The mind is going to say, "How?" Respond to the mind, "Just simply feel. When and where doesn't matter. I'll just feel." These are very simple natural

techniques. Little by little. It's not a competition. Taking what we're always already doing and just feeling it – feeling, not thinking. To feel is different than to think.

Connecting with the elements is an important step to connecting with the Great Spirit of Life. If in a natural way, we greet and respect the elements of nature, it will be easy to greet and thank God. Everything that exists is part of the Great Spirit of Life. Each one of us is a great creation of the Great Spirit of Life. Each one of us is part of that great whole. Depending on culture, epoch, etc, it's given different names. The words, the names don't matter. What's important is the connection with that Great Spirit of Life. It's the Great Spirit of Life that gives us life, and it's the Great Spirit of Life that is in the water and the other elements.

If we flow with love, together with the elements of nature that are tangible, that we can see, and that we have inside ourselves, if we flow with nature, without thinking, without worrying, we're going to flow in the wisdom of God. In my people's conception of God, God is not above or far away. God is in all places and in every moment. So we have many opportunities to be with the Great Spirit of Life – everywhere, all the time. We have many opportunities to be in permanent connection with the Great Wisdom of Life – with the Truth that is beyond the mind.

It's not true as history says that we worship the sun, the moon, the mountains. What they saw was the action of connection with the sun, moon, mountains, the action of respect and gratitude toward the elements of nature.

Through the connection with the elements we can perceive the Creator of Life. We can say, "I feel God". Then God goes from being something you think of to something you feel. To feel, to experience is what we need in this time. Believing may lead to fanaticism. Someone fanatical can become very dangerous. When we connect and feel the elements of nature, we feel some greatness. That feeling of greatness is feeling something about God. Then God won't be very far away. We'll feel God within us and everywhere.

If we feel God, we're neither near nor far from God. We realize we are part of God. If we experience

this, the words will not confuse us. We can describe a meal in various ways, but if we eat it, then we'll know. It won't be a belief. We'll know the taste.

In this moment, all of the power of Life is here. Within each one of you is the wisdom and power of Life. It's also in the air, the earth, the plants, the water, the sky, in every part of your body, in every aspect of this reality. Let's maintain the awareness of this power of Life, in ourselves and in everything, in order to elevate ourselves.

The invitation of the grandmothers and grandfathers is to feel everything, to capture the wisdom of everything. When we're running and rushing speedily and don't know to where, it's necessary to stop for a moment and feel – Life – to feel the air, the wind, the sun, the love of Mother Nature. This has a lot of value for life. Little by little as we continue to practice, we'll be filling ourselves. This is the spiritual path. This is the path of wisdom. This is the path of the wise.

Wisdom is like an innocence bathed in light. It's within each of us. This is the power that is attending our lives. A window or door to discover this power is feeling an element of nature. It makes us free like children are. It allows us to be free to fly like the birds.

Q: What wisdom are you referring to?

A: The wisdom is living with happiness.

We can read and listen to beautiful things. We may know about spiritual things, and know a lot of spiritual practices. Now, I invite you to live the spirituality each moment, through feeling. I invite you to be spiritual from within and everywhere. This is health; this is to be healed. Everything else is a technique or a therapy.

Health is in feeling, in living each moment, in being in continuous contact with the love of our Mother. That contact is ours to allow us to have access to the power of Life. That feeling allows us to discover the secrets of Life. We develop the power of feeling — more and more. It's not necessary to say, "I am spiritual. I have techniques." What's necessary is to live with feeling.

We're going to be happy. The spiritual is intimately involved with happiness. Reflection, meditation with permanent gratitude for life from the heart, gratitude for all the gifts life gives us in each moment, in each place — this is our way of living. There is no tomorrow in this way of living, benefiting each moment from the love of Mother Nature. It fills us immediately with gratitude. This is the deepest prayer without words – to feel immense gratitude for which words are very small. We'll see that the secrets of life have always been with us.

We're going to really be human beings, not products of people, but fully human beings. We're going to project towards others that light without having to do extraordinary things, just by being simple, by feeling. Yet when we touch and greet others, we're going to transmit that light, love, harmony and health. Then we are human beings. That is the invitation, that in every moment we become more human, feeling our heart, through feeling our life.

This does not mean, that in the path we're not going to find obstacles. Obstacles are very important.

Problems help us to have the opportunity to feel more, to understand other people. Every circumstance, every difficult situation has a gift within it, a well-guarded gift. The person who says, "I don't want any problems," perhaps doesn't want to receive the well-guarded gifts.

Life is a circle. If you did not open your gift at this point, then at another time, the same circumstance will come again. We must have gratitude for the difficulties and feel, "What is the gift? Where is the gift?" We must cry, and in the same way, we must laugh.

We must be like the water. It doesn't despair. It fills up and fills up until at a certain point it finds its way and then it produces other important things — like a beautiful waterfall — thanks to that obstacle. Or perhaps it makes a small lake or a lagoon, thanks to that obstacle.

Nature continuously teaches us how we must walk. The music is not in the instruments. The spiritual powers are not in the symbols. The power of crystal is not in the crystal. The power of the medium

of plants is not in the plants. These are only the packaging of the gifts. This body of flesh, bones and blood is a packaging only. The gift of each one is within.

This is my main intention – to remember the simple, plain things that have the power to transform our lives, that we can perform anytime. You can see that in simple things, there is wisdom. The keys are available everywhere and in all places. – places we might not think to look. We're looking way outside, but the keys are a lot closer to us than we realize. When I was a youth in this path, a friend was always saying, "I don't understand." One time a grandmother took him to the top of a mountain. "Look at what surrounds you, and tell me what you see." He started describing every detail of what he could see. She said, "Inside you is everything you just told me about."

There's a chant I want to teach you in Kichwa:

Tukuy shunkuan kuyanimi kikinda

With all my heart, I give you my love, unconditionally.

With these words the hands can gesture from being folded at the heart to being extended outward towards whatever you are greeting.

These words of loving with our whole heart express the attitude and feeling we need to have for all of life, for everything and everyone. We can use these words when we greet someone, or when we salute Mother Earth, or each of the four elements: fire, wind, water, earth. Anything our eyes see, we can greet and thank. This is very important.

The elements of nature are wherever we are. They are what we are.

We are one in the love of Mother Nature and the Great Spirit of Life.

Feeling this oneness, this love, brings fulfillment and happiness to our lives.

This is the wisdom, this is the experience, that comes from friendship with the elements. May you experience this, every day, more and more.

Essentials

Helen Slomovits

The fewer the words —
The better I remember, the more I can savor the teaching.
The briefer the instruction —
The more I can make the experience my own.
The simpler the practice —
The more likely I am to <u>do</u> it.
The more repetitive the assignment —
The more I can see myself reflected in its mirror.

Earth, Air, Fire, Water —
The practice of becoming intimate with these,
Inside and outside
The practice of giving thanks to these,
Inside and outside
Leaves no moment, no place — empty.

Each moment, each place — an opportunity
To offer gratitude —
for each breath, for each bite, for each step, for each sight
To connect —
with water gliding down my throat as I drink, down my skin as I shower,
with the rain, with a river
To fill myself with happiness
with the smooth solidity of a river stone,
with the treasured, brief palette of fall colors,
with a hanging mist that turns the familiar into mystery

Each moment — sacred
Each place — sacred
Each moment, each place — a chance to give thanks
For all I've been given
For all I've <u>not</u> been given (an unexpected catalyst for joy!)
In this wonderful, wild dance with Life.

Afterword

In childhood I experienced a natural love of and connection with nature, and many times found solace in its healing power. Though my love of nature didn't go away as an adult, little by little, without my even being aware of it, my priorities and lifestyle took me away from the daily connection and intimacy I'd felt as a child. As I woke up to this reality, I felt a deep sense of grief and loss.

In 1999, in answer to a silent prayer, I was given the opportunity to meet Don Alverto Taxo, and since then I've attended numerous workshops in the US and traveled three times to Ecuador. Learning with Don Alverto is always immediate, intimate and full of heart. Through him I've come to regard the elements — earth, air, fire, water — as friends with whom I share love, gifts and exchanges of feeling, and from whom I receive healing. Little by little, step by step, awareness of the elements in each moment and each place, in the simplest of daily tasks — is bringing me home to my heart and grounding me in my body. More and more I find myself able to experience the intimate connection with myself, with other people and with each form of life I encounter. And this brings love, appreciation and satisfaction moment to moment, as I live my life. For this, and for encouraging me to express through music the feelings of my heart, I am deeply grateful to Don Alverto.

It's my intention and desire that you, too, experience how very natural and easy it is to connect with the elements, with Nature, and with the Great Spirit of Life. My prayer is that you feel drawn to explore and find for yourself, your own way of being intimate with the elements, and come to feel yourself as part of Nature, not separate from Her. May the power and immediacy of Don Alverto's words, light the path of intimate friendship with the elements for you.

Helen Slomovits